William Henry Dalrymple

The name of Dalrymple:

With the genealogy of one branch of the family in the United States

William Henry Dalrymple

The name of Dalrymple:
With the genealogy of one branch of the family in the United States

ISBN/EAN: 9783337727659

Printed in Europe, USA, Canada, Australia, Japan

Cover: Foto ©ninafisch / pixelio.de

More available books at **www.hansebooks.com**

THE
NAME OF
DALRYMPLE:

WITH THE

GENEALOGY

OF ONE BRANCH OF THE FAMILY

IN THE

UNITED STATES.

BY W. H. DALRYMPLE.

HAVERHILL, MASS.
PRINTED BY THE AUTHOR.
1878.

THE NAME OF
DALRYMPLE.

According to the best information I have been able to obtain, I think the name was originally spelled De La Rumple; and that a family of that name resided in some part of France. About four hundred years ago, or somewhere between the years 1450 and 1500 some persons of that name emigrated from France to Scotland, and there the name was soon after changed to Dalrymple, and has so continued to the present time. The name is rather a common one, both in Scotland and England, and has attained to honorable distinction in the history of the British nation, as any one may discover by consulting almost any of the English encyclopedias.

Not far from the year 1730 a gentleman by the name of Dalrymple emigrated from Scotland to this country, bringing with him two sons, Robert and Thomas, who were then but

young lads. Whether the family settled in Sudbury, Mass. immediately on their arrival in this country, or not, I have not been able to ascertain, but it is quite certain that they were living there not many years after their landing in this country. Robert, while yet a young man, and unmarried, left his home to seek his fortune in New Hampshire, then comparatively a wilderness, with towns very small, and at a long distance from each other, and most of them quite destitute of any postal accommodations. No tidings were received from him by his family after he left home, and his long absence continued to be a mystery through that and the next generation. But in the year 1858, being in the town of Bedford, N. H. I there met with a history of that town, and in it discovered the name of Robert Dalrymple as one of the town's quota of soldiers, sent to Canada in the old French and Indian war. It was also stated in that connection, that he was one of the missing who never returned, and from whom no intelligence was afterwards received. The name

was not spelt as it is at present, but I recognized it as acording to the old Scotch pronunciation—Delrumple.

Thomas Dalrymple, as I have been informed by Mrs. Coggswell, his grand-daughter, had five children, Sally and Polly, James, John and Thomas. Sally married a Fovel and lived in Boston. She had two children, Eliza and John, both of whom lived to grow up, but died rather young. Polly married a Pratt, and had two daughters, Polly, who married a Gay, and Patty, who married a Pettee; but where they lived, and how long, I have not the means of knowing. Mrs. Fovel died about the year 1810.

Thomas' three sons all served more or less in the war of the Revolution. John returned to his father's house in Sudbury at the close of the war, and died soon after. Thomas was in a regiment captured by the British, and nothing was heard of him afterwards. It was supposed, however, by his friends, that he died a prisoner of war in some one of the British prisons.

James, the oldest son of Thomas, was born March 4, 1757. He remained at home, working on the farm with his father, I think, till the opening scenes of the the Revolution. In June, 1775, when a call was made for troops to go to Cambridge and Charlestown, he was among the first in town to respond to that call, and, although but little more than eighteen years old, shouldered his musket, and started at once for the seat of war. He arrived at Cambridge and reported himself ready for duty in the service of his country. He was assigned to a company which received orders to march that night to Charlestown and fortify Bunker's Hill. He assisted in preparing the fort on the night of the 16th of June, and in defending it against the attack of the British on the 17th. He fought bravely with his companions until for want of ammunition they had orders to retreat.

I have several times in my youthful days heard him relate his adventures in the war, and, particularly, his experience in getting away from the Hill in the confusion of retreat.

When the order was given to retreat, and he saw that his services could no longer be of any avail in the fort, his next thought was to look out for his own safety in the best way he could, and he rushed out of the fort just as the British were about to enter it. As he left the sally-port he saw a fine looking horse with saddle and bridle standing near the fort. Not seeing any one who appeared to have charge of the horse, he thought what a fine thing it would be to ride down the hill instead of using his own legs. He stepped up to the horse and took hold of the bridle in order to mount him, when a British officer on the opposite side, whom he had not till that moment discovered, sprang forward and says, "What are you going to do with that horse?" to which he made the laconic reply, "Nothing," and immediately started down the hill upon a run. In descending the hill he came to a fence, and as he was stepping over it two bullets struck the upper rail, one on each side of him, and but few inches distant. They only served, however, to quicken his pace as he

jumped from the fence and continued to run in the direction taken by those ahead of him till he was beyond the range of British muskets, and in company of his retreating companions. With a sharp lookout in the rear, they continued their retreat until they came to Charlestown Neck. Here the balls from the Glasgow, a British man-of-war, and some gondolas which were stationed in the river, were sweeping across the Neck almost incessantly. He, however, with many others, passed over unharmed, and reached Cambridge that night in safety. He then enlisted during the war, and being a good drummer he afterwards served in that capacity; and having served his country faithfully through that dark and trying period, and having been engaged in numerous battles with the enemy, without being seriously injured, he received an honorable discharge at the close of the war, and returned to his father's house, to cultivate the soil, and rest from the fatigues of the camp. For many years, in the latter part of his life, he received a soldier's pension.

On the first day of December, 1780, probably while at home on a furlough, he was married to Azubah Parmenter of Sudbury, Mass.

She was born January 26, 1764, and was a lineal descendant of Samuel Maverick, who figured somewhat conspicuously in the early history of Boston, and whose name is still perpetuated in the public buildings and streets of that city. She was a noble woman, of a strong and vigorous constitution, and with a kind and gentle heart, in which the motherly feelings largely predominated.

Some years after their marriage he bought a farm in Framingham, in a neighborhood known as Salem End. He lived here till the spring of 1819, cultivating the land in the summer, and making boots and shoes in the winter. He then sold his farm in Framingham, and purchased another in the north part of Marlborough near to Stow. Here he lived till within a few years of his death, when, through the infirmities of age, he was no longer capable of managing his farm; and he and his wife went to live with their daughters.

He died in the family of his youngest daughter in Leominster, on the 5th day of July, 1847, at the age of ninety years and four months. She survived him a little more than three years, and died on the 12th of August, 1850; in the eighty-seventh year of her age.

They had lived together from the time of their marriage, almost sixty-seven years; had been members of the first Baptist church in Framingham between thirty and forty years, and lived and died respected and beloved by all who knew them. They had nine children, only two of whom were living at the time of their death.

THE CHILDREN OF JAMES AND AZUBAH DALRYMPLE.

1. William Dalrymple, son of James, was born October 31, 1781. After spending his minority mostly at home with his father, he engaged in some business transactions in Canada, which required frequent journeys between Quebec and Montreal. In one of these journeys, he, with one or two companions,

was overtaken by a violent snow-storm, when
far from any human habitation, and he perished from fatigue and the intense cold on the
14th of December, 1811. He was unmarried.

II. Henry Dalrymple, son of James, was
born July 13, 1784. He learned the trade of
a cooper, and worked at it some time in Watertown, Ms. He was married in 1807, (the
exact date I have not been able to obtain,) to
Catherine Tileston of Dorchester, Ms. She
was born in Dorchester, June 20, 1781.

Not long after his marriage, he gave up
his business in Watertown, and, with his
brother-in-law, Samuel Clark, leased a tavern stand in Waltham, where he remained only a few years, and then moved to Cambridgeport, and resumed his business as a cooper.

He had lived here but a year or two when
the second war with England commenced,
and he soon enlisted into the service, and went
with a company from Cambridgeport. He
was in several engagements in the vicinity of
the lakes, and received his death wound near

a fort situated on a point of land formed by the entrance of the Oswego river into Lake Ontario. He received two wounds almost at the same time. In one case the ball entered his mouth, carrying away his front teeth, badly cutting his tongue, and passed out at the back part of his neck, a little on one side of the bones. Strange as it may seem, that wound soon healed, so that he was able to take food with comparative comfort. In the other case, the wound of which he died, the ball entered the upper part of the thigh, penetrating the bone just below the hip joint. The surgeons made an unsuccessful attempt to extract the ball, and he died of mortification on the twenty-second day of May, two weeks and two days from the time he received the wound. He left three sons, the oldest at the time of his death being a little more than six years, and the youngest sixteen months.

His widow lived forty-five years after his death, and died May 6, 1859, the same day of the month on which he received his death wound. She was a member of the Baptist

church in Neponset, Dorchester, at the time of her death, and had been for many years.

She was a good wife and mother, and endeavored to bring up her children in the nurture and admonition of the Lord. In her old age she was tenderly cared for by her youngest son, and died at his house in Dorchester.

III. Asenath Dalrymple, daughter of James, was born September 1, 1786. She married, 1st, Samuel Clark of Framingham, November 25, 1806. By this marriage she had one daughter, who was her only child.

Mr. Clark kept a public house a few years, was engaged in farming several years, and died in Framingham, August 29, 1833.

She married, 2d, Josiah Randall of Stow, May 7, 1835. He died September 11, 1844, leaving her in possession of a large and valuable farm, in the southerly part of Stow, on what is called "Boon's Hill."

About two years after the death of Mr. Randall she married, 3d, Samuel Mead, who came and lived with her, but his death occur-

ring a few years after their marriage, she was again left a widow, but in full possession of her farm. Here she continued to live until admonished by the infirmities of advancing age, that she should seek to be relieved from some of the cares and burdens of life. She then sold her farm, and went to live with her daughter, Mrs. Parker, in Medfield, where she died, February 10, 1873.

IV. Ezekiel Dalrymple, son of James, was born April 15, 1789. He was inclined to a sea-faring life, and after following that occupation several years, he went to South America, and engaged in privateering. He sailed as master of a vessel from some port, I think, in the southern part of Brazil, in the month of May, 1819. Soon after the vessel left port, a violent storm arose, and neither the vessel, nor any of the crew, was afterwards heard from. He was unmarried.

V. John Dalrymple, son of James, was born February 26, 1792. He learned the

trade of a shoemaker, and spent the early part of his life at home with his father, cultivating the land in the summer, and at work at his trade in the winter. He married, June 9, 1822, Judith Loring of Cohasset, and soon after went into business in Boston, where he accumulated some property, and owned a house in North Russell st. Here he continued to live till his death, which occurred September 22, 1830. He left two sons; and the widow, with her children, continued to reside at No. 10, North Russell st., where the boys enjoyed all the advantages of the Boston schools till they had become qualified for business, after which they purchased a house at Newton Corner, where the family continued to reside for many years. The mother died in 1853, but I have not the exact date.

VI. James Dalrymple jr., son of James, was born January 11 1796. He lived at the old homestead mostly through his minority, when he became quite a proficient in the art of dancing, and taught the same very success-

fully several years in Boston and the vicinity.

He married Sophia Warren of Brighton, and resided there several years. He afterwards went to Austerlitz, N. Y., where he died, August 28, 1835; leaving several children, but how many, and their names, I have no means of knowing.

VII. Ann Dalrymple, daughter of James, was born April 16, 1798. She lived at home with her parents, and being quite ingenious, produced some very fine specimens of straw-work in the way of bonnets, as well as needle work of great variety. She possesed a very gentle and affectionate disposition, and, although she has now been dead more than fifty years, yet memory, faithful and true, presents her even now most vividly before my mind, with that beautiful, but indescribable smile, which always lighted up her countenance so lovingly at every meeting with her friends.

She died of dysentery, after two weeks of painful sickness, September 5, 1825.

VIII. Sally Dalrymple, daughter of James, was born May 26, 1800. She is said to have been a very beautiful child, and apparently in the enjoyment of excellent health, until suddenly smitten down by the spotted fever, which, after a few days of severe sickness, terminated in death, April 7, 1810.

IX Eliza Dalrymple, daughter of James, was born October 31, 1806. She qualified herself for teaching, and became quite successful in that vocation, having taught many terms in the vicinity of the old homestead, in the north part of Marlborough, much to the satisfaction of parents and children. She was married October 10, 1832, to Seth Coggswell of Leominster, Mass., and went there to live, leaving the old hive almost emty. Her parents were then quite aged, with no one of their children to come to their aid.

Mr. Coggswell was born in Lunenburg, February 21, 1798, where he continued to reside through the early part of his life; then purchased a farm in the northern part of

Leominster, where he spent the remainder of his days, and died March 27, 1877. His widow still survives him, and lives at the old homestead in Leominster with some of her children. He and his wife were both worthy members of the Methodist Episcopal church, and he was for many years a local preacher in that denomination.

CHILDREN OF HENRY, 2D SON OF JAMES, AND CATHERINE DALRYMPLE.

1 William Henry Dalrymple was born in Watertown, Mass., February 20, 1808.

After his father's death, and when he was about seven and a half years old, his mother placed him in the care of a farmer by the name of James Greenwood, in the south part of Framingham, where he was very kindly cared for by the family till he was sixteen years of age, when his mother, thinking it might be better for him to learn a trade, made arrangements for him to learn the watchmaker's trade with Fisher Metcalf esq., of Hopkinton, Ms.

After working at that business one year he became dissatisfied, and obtained permission to return to his former home in the Greenwood family. Here he continued to reside during the remainder of his minority, enjoying the advantages of the public schools, and sometimes the fall term at the academy, in the centre of the town.

On the fifth day of September, 1830, he was baptized by the Rev. Charles Train, and received into the first Baptist church in Framingham. He taught one of the district schools here two winters in succession, and in the spring of 1831 commenced a course of study preparatory for the christian ministry. After two years of preparatory study, he entered the Theological Institution at Newton, in the class which entered in 1833, and after spending nearly two years with the class, his health became so much impaired by study, that he felt it a duty to leave for a few months.

Just at that time he received a request from the committee of the Baptist church in South Abington, Ms. to supply their pulpit a few

sabbaths, with which he complied, and soon after, the church sent him a unanimous invitation to become their pastor. This he accepted, and was ordained April 29, 1835.

On the ninth day of July, 1835, he was married to Elizabeth Adams of Boston. She was born in West Cambridge, July 25, 1814, and is a descendant from the same family of Adamses which furnished Samuel, the mainspring of the Revolution, and John, and John Quincy, both presidents of the United States.

For more than forty years she has followed with her husband the leadings of Providence, when the pathway of life has seemed dark and mysterious, with a fortitude and fidelity which well becomes a good soldier of the cross.

In the first decade, or ten years of his ministry, he preached in the following places in Mass. South Abington, two years; the two churches in Deerfield and Shelburn, as a missionary, one year; Northborough two years; South Gardner two years; and Manchaug, in Sutton, one year. In the second decade he preached in Woodville, in Hopkinton, two

years; and two years he was lecturing and collecting agent for the American Peace Society. About a year and a half he supplied a church in Barnstable, and from there he went to Fitzwilliam, N. H. and preached between two and three years, and one year in Merrimack. In the third decade he was with the church in Hudson three years, and Stratham two; then moved to East Haverhill, Mass. where he preached four years.

At the end of this period his health had so far failed that he did not feel able to take the pastoral care of another church. In April, 1867, he moved to Georgetown, where he lived four years, supplying churches in different places, as opportunity presented. In the spring of 1871 he went to Bradford, and lived on Pleasant st. three and a half years, and from February to August, 1872, preached to a small colored church in that town. In the fall of 1874 he moved to 28 Green st., Haverhill, where he still lives, but in a very poor state of health, and has been for the last seven or eight years.

He preached his first sermon in the Baptist church in West Dedham, October 30, 1831, and his last in Portland st. church, Haverhill, June 1, 1873. And the whole number of sermons preached, from first to last, is 3693, besides, probably, conducting as many prayer and conference meetings in the same time.

2 Albert Dalrymple was born in Waltham, Mass., November 1, 1810. He was about three and a half years old at the time of his father's death, and continued with his mother till he was about eight years old, when he went to live with an old gentleman in Framingham, by the name of Reuben Torrey, who had a small farm which he cultivated in the summer and in the winter worked at shoemaking. Being in a good neighborhood, and near to a good school, he enjoyed, in these particulars, quite superior advantages. He remained with Mr. Torrey until he was about sixteen or seventeen years of age, when his mother placed him with a Mr. Adams of Dorchester, to learn the cabinet-makers trade.

After serving his time through with Mr. Adams, he spent some time in Boston, working at his trade, then went to Baltimore, Md., where he remained about a year, and then returned to Boston, and went to work at the piano-forte business, principally at making cases, at which he continued many years.

He was married, November 26, 1838, to Emeline Smith of Boston, and continued to reside there till his wife's health becoming very poor, he moved to Melrose, where, on the fourth day of May, 1870, after a lingering sickness, she died of consumption. Soon after her death, his own health being poor, he was at length obliged to relinquish his business, and went to reside with his oldest son, a silver-plater in Boston.

3 James Tileston Dalrymple was born in Cambridgeport, January 8, 1813. Soon after his father's death, the family moved to Framingham, and he continued with his mother till about nine or ten years old, when

he went to live in the family of Mr. Greenwood, who had so kindly taken an interest in his older brother. When about sixteen years of age he went to Dorchester, to learn the currying business of E. & I. Field, who at that time carried on quite an extensive business on the upper road. Thinking it would be a better location for their business, as well as more convenient, they afterwards moved to the lower road, and established their business at the place since known as Field's Corner. After serving out his apprenticeship with them, he continued in their employ many years more; and feeling inclined to make that place his permanent home, he purchased a small house, and, with his mother, continued to reside there till her death, which occurred in 1859, and some years after. Not having any family of his own, and his health being not as good as in former years, he concluded it would be better for him to leave his house, and board in some family. Accordingly he went into the family of a neighbor, where he still continues. He has never married.

THE FAMILY OF SAMUEL CLARK, AND ASENATH DALRYMPLE CLARK.

Mary Clark was their only child, and was born November 22, 1807. She lived at home with her parents until about eighteen or twenty years of age, when she went to Boston and learned the tailor's trade, but did not have an opportunity to work at it very long, for on September 30, 1830, she was married to Blake Parker of Southboro'.

About the time of his marriage he went to Medfield and engaged in the staging and express busines between Medfield and Boston. When the rail-road was opened to Dedham, he drove his stage to that place, taking passengers on the way, then took the cars for Boston, returning in the afternoon by the same route. This business he followed diligently and faithfully through life.

He left rather a numerous family, some of whom remain in Medfield, and others scattered in various directions. One son took the business of father, and continues to follow it.

THE FAMILY OF JOHN DALRYMPLE, AND JUDITH LORING DALRYMPLE.

1 Austin Webster Dalrymple was born in Boston, April 13, 1823. He lived in Boston with his parents, and after completing the regular course in the grammar school, he went into a dry goods store, first as an errand boy, then as a salesman, in which business he continued through life. When he was but little more than twenty-one years of age, the family purchased a house at Newton Corner, and went there to reside, renting their former residence in Boston. He still continued at his business in Boston, going in on the cars in the morning, and returning in the evening. He had followed this practice for many years, when, on the evening of October 19, 1859, in attempting to step upon a train after it had commenced moving, he slipped, or in some way lost his foothold, and fell upon the track between the cars, two or three of which passed over his body, and he was instantly killed.

He was married, and left a wife, and, I

think, several children, but how many I am not informed.

2 George Lafayette Dalrymple was born in Boston, June 19, 1825. With his brother he attended the public schools, and afterwards learned the painter's trade, which he followed for several years in Boston and the vicinity. He then went to California and spent a few years, when he made a brief visit of a few weeks to his friends in the east, returning again to California; since which no tidings have been received from him, nor concerning him, by his friends, and it is now generally supposed that he is dead, probably dying among strangers, and perhaps very suddenly, leaving no communication for his friends. He was never married, unless he was married after he went to California the last time.

Nothing can be said concerning the family of James Dalrymple jr., in addition to what has already been said on the sixteenth page of this book.

THE FAMILY OF SETH COGGSWELL, AND ELIZA DALRYMPLE COGGSWELL.

1 Francis Rodolphus Coggswell was born December 1, 1833. He was married September 12, 1876, and has resided for several years in the city of New Orleans, Ala.

2 James Dalrymple Coggswell was born October 26, 1835. He resides at the old homestead, and has charge of the farm, thus endeavoring, as far as possible, to repair the loss to the family, occasioned by the death of his honored father.

3 Ann Parmenter Coggswell was born December 16, 1838; and died March 12, 1841.

4 Angeline Eliza Coggswell was born February 1, 1842. Like a dutiful daughter, she followed the example of a worthy mother, and commenced teaching at quite an early age, and has followed the profession with so much success, that her services have been in constant requisition since.

5 George Webster Coggswell was born

March 29, 1844. He was married January 4, 1871, and now resides in the town of Shrewsbury, Mass.

6 Martha Charlena Coggswell was born March 12, 1848.

THE FAMILY OF WILLIAM HENRY DALRYMPLE, AND ELIZABETH ADAMS DALRYMPLE.

1 Henry Augustus Dalrymple was born in South Abington, Mass., October 1, 1836.

He passed the earlier years of his life attending to such duties and employments, as generally fall to the lot of boys to perform, until sixteen years of age, when, on the eleventh day of the following April, he first left home to see what he could do for himself, and entered the employ of Wheeler & March, dry goods dealers in Watertown, Mass., as a clerk in their store. The business not fully meeting his expectations, a change was effected and he next found himself in the city of Boston, working at the stamp gilding business.

During the month of September, of the

same year, 1853, he went to Fitchburg, Ms. where he commenced working for Charles Johnson, at the bookbinder's trade, which he has followed in Boston, Lowell, Lancaster and Lawrence, Mass. In this last place he was partner and joint proprietor in the business. In April, 1871, he accepted a situation as foreman, and general manager of the bindery in connection with the office of the "Nashua Telegraph"; which position he still occupies, October, 1878.

From February 4, 1865, to February 4, 1869, he gave up the business in consequence of ill health, and during these four years, he devoted a large portion of his time to the instruction of children in the science of vocal music. He taught juvenile classes in East Haverhill, West Newbury, Byfield, Newburyport and Georgetown, Ms., and gave public concerts in each of these places, with his pupils. He also gave public concerts with the same pupils, in West Amesbury, (now Merrimac,) and Haverhill city, sixteen concerts in all.

In the Fall of 1867, he, with his sister Mary, receiving a very cordial invitation from Col. R. N. Temple, agent of the "Original Father Kemp's Old Folks Concert Company" to join them, they entered their ranks, and that season travelled some twelve hundred miles, in all the New England states, except Vermont. But the trip proving unsuccessful financially, it was given up in December.

On the first Sabbath in the year, January 2, 1870, he was baptized by his father, and united with the second Baptist church in the city of Lawrence.

August 14, of the same year, he was married by his father at Georgetown, to Miss Amelia Hannah Leach, of Lawrence.

Her native place was West Boylston, Ms. and she was born December 22, 1850.

January 3, 1878, he was elected junior deacon of the first Baptist church in Nashua, N. H.

2 Ellen Maria Dalrymple was born in Northborough, May 3, 1839. During a revival of religion, which occurred in Hudson,

N. H. in the summer of 1856, when her father was pastor of the Baptist church in that place, quite a number of young people professed conversion, and united with that church. She was one of that number, and was baptized by her father, October 19, of the same year. January 19, 1876, she was married, by her father, to Joseph H. Bousley, of Salem, Mass., and went there to reside. She has one son, Willie Dalrymple Bousley, who was born May 3, 1877.

3 Mary Elizabeth Dalrymple was born in South Gardner, Mass., January 24, 1842.

She remained at home with her parents, mostly through life, having never married, and, with her sisters, enlivened the home circle with music and song. She had naturally a very generous disposition, and being very industrious in her habits, she earned considerable money, which she freely parted with, when she thought it would contribute in any way to the comfort or enjoyment of her parents, or other friends. She had quite a superior musical talent, and, for four years

previous to her death, she was the leading soprano singer in the choir of the Portland st. Baptist church, Haverhill.

In August, 1875, she was taken suddenly sick, and after several months of severe sickness, her disease terminated in consumption, in which she lingered through the following summer, and died December 28, 1876.

The following lines were inserted, in connection with a notice of her death, in the WATCHMAN, January 11, 1877.

> Long will the fragrance of her memory dwell
> In many a heart that knew and loved her well;
> For others' good, more than her own, she thought,
> And till the last with weary fingers wrought.

4 Sarah Jennie Dalrymple was born in Hopkinton, Mass. February 26, 1844. She was inclined from a very early age to read and study books, and draw designs on slate or paper, and would often amuse herself in this way for hours at a time. While the family resided in Nashua, N. H. for two or three years, she very diligently improved the

educational advantages afforded by the city schools, and when the family left the place in 1860, she had a good record in the Mount Pleasant High School. When the family afterwards went to East Haverhill, Mass., she soon received an appointment as teacher in one of the public schools, and taught there several successive terms. She, like her older sister, has a very fine musical taste, and can play skilfully on the piano or the organ, but has not the clear, strong vocal power for singing, which her older sister had.

December 22, 1870, she was married by her father, assisted by the Rev. D. D. Marsh, pastor of the Peabody Memorial Church in Georgetown, to Richmond Barbour Root, M. D. a young physician, who had then but recently commenced practice in that place, where she has since continued to reside.

5   Katie Adams Dalrymple was born in Neponset village, Dorchester, since annexed to the city of Boston, February 13, 1851.

She spent her life mostly at home, the light and joy of the family circle. She had

a peculiar faculty for acquiring knowledge in almost any bransh of education, and made rapid, as well as thorough proficiency in all her studies, graduating at the High School in Georgetown, February 25, 1870. Soon after her graduation, she was appointed a teacher in one of the public schools, but, after teach- a few terms, her health began to fail, and it was evident that her strength was not equal to the task of teaching, and she gave it up.

She, also, had a very delicate ear for music, and could play at sight, on the piano or organ, almost any piece of music with great accuracy; and at the time she was taken ill with her last sickness, she was engaged to supply the place of the organist of the Portland st. Baptist church for a few weeks, that she might be absent.

Msy 19, 1872, she was baptized by Rev. A. J. Padelford, and received into the membership of the Portland st. Baptist church.

April 20, 1873, she went to meeting as usual and played the organ through the day, and at the close of the afternoon service, she

remained an hour or more to play for a rehersal by the choir. At the close of that service, from the exercise at the organ, and the heat of the house, her clothes had become damp with perspiration, and in that condition she left the church, and walked home, about three forths of a mile, in a cold wind, the weather having changed to very much colder since morning. That was the last Sabbath she ever went to meeting. A slow, lingering fever followed that exposure, and this terminated in consumption, of which she died, April 16, 1874.

6 Joseph Adams Dalrymple was born in Hudson, N. H. April 26, 1858. For various reasons he did not have so good an opportunity to attend the public schools at the age when children usually make their first appearance in the school-room, as the other members of the family had, and until he was six or seven years of age, his education was managed chiefly in the family, and by his sisters. In April, 1867, the family moved to Georgetown, where the schools were well

graded, and in very good condition. When he first entered the public schools in Georgetown, being then scarcely nine years old, he was placed with boys of a similar age in the primary department. He had been there but a few weeks, when his teacher informed the committe that he did not belong in her department, as he was evidently too far advanced in his studies to be benefited in her classes, and advised that he be sent to the grammar school, in the room above. He entered the first year, or lowest class of the grammar school, and, after a short time was advanced to the second year, and then went through the regular course, and in the spring of 1870, entered the High School in that town.

In the spring of 1871 the course of his studies was somewhat interrupted in consequence of the family moving from Georgetown to Bradford. He lost no time, however, as he entered the Bradford High School in the second year, and graduated on the second day of July, 1874, with the second honors of his class, the salutatory in Latin.

On the first of September, of the same year, he entered on a four years course of training in the druggist and apothecary establishment of Emerson & Howe, in Haverhill, Mass. where he still continues, (Nov. 1, 1878) and for more than two years past, has been head clerk in that popular and reliable house.

After the 25th page of this book had been printed, I received a communication from Mrs. Parker, of Medfield, giving quite a full account of her own family, together with some statistics in regard to her father's family, which I had not before in my possession.

From this I obtain the following additional particulars, viz:

Samuel Clark was born in Hopkinton, Ms. May 11, 1778.

Samuel Mead, of Boxboro', and Asenath Randall, of Stow, were married March 7, 1847.

Blake Parker was born in Southboro', December 10, 1806, and died in Medfield, August 27, 1871.

THE FAMILY OF BLAKE PARKER, AND MARY C. PARKER.

For about two or three years after their marriage, the family resided in Southboro', but business prospects of a flattering character presenting themselves at Medfield. Mr. Parker was induced to improve the opportunity, and he moved to that town about forty-five years ago, where he spent the remainder of his days, and where many of his family still continue to reside.

1 Alonzo Blake Parker was born in Southborough, March 15, 1832. (All the other children were born in Medfield.) He married Anna Day Knapp, of Cumberland, R. I. September 24, 1857.

2 Ann Eliza Parker was born October 30, 1833. She married Lewis Hartshorn, of Medford, October 23, 1853. He died July 25, 1878.

3 George Frederick Parker was born January 25, 1836. He married Marinda Osgood, of Milford, May 7, 1856.

4 Frances Dolly Parker was born March 3, 1839.

5 Henry Marshall Parker was born September 13 1840. He married, 1, Charlotte Arathusa Wright. She died January 28, 1871. He married, 2, Maria Louise Hall, of Johnson, Vt. June 6, 1875.

6 Ellen Mary Parker was born April 22, 1845

7 Herbert Eugene Parker was born October 27, 1846.

THE FAMILY OF HENRY AUGUSTUS DALRYMPLE, AND AMELIA H. LEACH DALRYMPLE.

1 Mabel Elizabeth Dalrymple was born in Lawrence, Mass. June 17, 1871.

2 Henry Raymond Dalrymple was born in Nashua, N. H. June 4, 1874.

3 Rollin Adams Dalrymple was born in Nashua, N. H. July 8, 1878.

THE FAMILY OF RICHMOND B. ROOT M. D. AND S. JENNIE DALRYMPLE ROOT.

1 Roy Richmond Root was born in Georgetown, Mass. September 30, 1873. He died June 8, 1876.

2 Katie Dalrymple Root was born in Georgetown, Mass. December 17, 1874.

3 May Barbour Root was born in Georgetown, Mass. April 25, 1877.

NOTE.— If any one wishes to trace the line of the oldest son through the foregoing pages, he will find that Henry Raymond is the oldest son of Henry Augustus; that Henry Augustus is the oldest son of William Henry; that William Henry is the oldest son of Henry; that Henry was the oldest son, who had any family, of James; that James was the oldest son of Thomas; that Thomas was the oldest son, who had any family, of his father, so far as I can discover; and beyond that I have no positive and reliable light to guide me in this matter.

CORRECTIONS.

Omissions and errors are not uncommon, even among experienced and practical printers, therefore, a person who never received any personal instruction in the art, and has had but very little experience in the same, may with some confidence hope for the par- of his readers for the blunders they may discover.

The following lines, which appeared in the WATCHMAN AND REFLECTOR, in connection with a notice of the death of Katie A. Dalrymple, should have been inserted at the close of the sketch given of her on page 36, but being mislaid at the time, were omitted.

> Farewell, dear one, all pain and sorrow o'er,
> In thy bright home, where death intrudes no more,
> Thine is the joy the crown of life to wear,
> Be ours the joy one day to meet thee there.

On page 17, supply p in emty.
On page 28, line 6 Ala. should be La.
Other similar errors the intelligent reader will be able to correct as he meets with them.

Conclusion.

I was induced to undertake the preparation of this little work at the suggestion of my oldest son, who had often heard me speak of my grandparents and their family in his youthful days, and who thought that some connected account of the name and family ought to be preserved in a more permanent and reliable form than tradition.

And as I am among the very few that remain, who were personally acquainted with the former generation, and who know something of their personal history, such circumstances seemed to point to me as the one to do the work, if it was ever to be done.

In looking back over a period of fifty or sixty years, my memory may have been a little faulty in some instances, but it has been my first endeavor that every statement and record should be as accurate as possible.

This book, of course, will be interesting or attractive only to such persons as bear the Name, or are in some way connected with it, therefore I have printed but a small edition,

sixty copies in all, which I propose to scatter among the families bearing the name, or who may be nearly related to it.

When I commenced the work last September, it was with many doubts whether I should live to complete it, for my health was so poor, that while I was able some days to work four or five hours, on others I could work only an hour, or a part of one, and many days was not able to do even that.

But through the great mercy, and lovingkindness of my heavenly Father, who has watched over me, and kept and blest me all my days, I have been enabled to bring it to a close, except what I may add in an appendix.

Haverhill, Mass. November 15, 1878.

APPENDIX.

The following is a copy of a letter from Capt. Rufus McIntire, esq. who was in command of the company of which my father, Henry Dalrymple, was clerk and orderly sergeant at the time he received his fatal wounds. Capt. McIntire settled in Parsonsfield, Me. soon after the war as [   ] and remained there in the practice of his profession through life, fifty years or more.

The letter was written to James T. Dalrymple, my brother, in answer to some inquiries made by him.

Parsonsfield, Me. Nov. 21, 1860.
Mr. James T. Dalrymple:

Dear Sir. Yours of the 19th inst. was received last evening.

Nothing affords me greater pleasure than to renew an acquaintance with my companions in the war of 1812, now few in number, and much scattered, or to make the acquaint-

ance of their descendants. Your letter furnishes me with the first intelligence I have had for nearly half a century of the family of your lamented father, my companion and friend, sergeant Dalrymple. My letter, written soon after the melancholy event of his death, probably gave more accurate information of the facts than my memory could now furnish, though many incidents that transpired are still fresh in my recollection as though of yesterday. Oswego presented at the time of the battle a very different picture from the present.

The fort where the fight took place was on a bluff, on the east side of the mouth of the river, and on the point formed by the river and the lake shore. The land about it was a plain common. A glen shot to the east, extending up the river half a mile, perhaps, and bordered east and south by a young growth of bushes. There was no inhabited house for nearly half a mile, and then one or two at the ferry, and at the foot of the rapids.

The village was on the west side of the river, extending from above the ferry nearly

to a point opposite the fort. I was told many years ago, that this common was covered with streets and houses, and at the ferry an extensive flouring establishment was erected.

The wounded men were carried to the house at the ferry. Who lived there I do not recollect, if I ever knew. We had to retreat to the falls, twelve miles above, and remained there till we marched to Sackett's Harbor, though I occasionally visited Oswego, and the sick and wounded men.

Probably the lady that wrote about your father's death occupied the house. Volney may have been the name of the town on the east side of the river, it was, I recollect, in a different county from Oswego on the other side of the river. There was, probably, some place near the old fort used as a burying-ground when the fort was garrisoned in former times, but I do not recollect whether your father was buried on that side of the river, or carried over to the village graveyard, if they had one. I cannot now say whether any monument was erected at your

father's grave. It was not easy at that time to get suitable stones for such purposes in that wild country Lieut. Blaney was killed in that battle, and the subject of grave-stones was discussed. I have seen printed accounts stating that stones were erected by the officers. If this was so, it is probable stones were also erected at your father's grave.

Such have been the changes there, from a naked, barren common to a large village, or city of extensive manufactories and trade, that I doubt if any vestages now remain of the fortification burying-ground.

The battle, I think, took place early in the afternoon. Your father received his first wound in the hip or thigh, which was the fatal one. I left him on the field, on retreat, perhaps a quarter of a mile from the fort.

Soon after I looked back and saw Col. Mitchell, the only mounted officer, off his horse. I returned back to see what was the matter, and to assist him if necessary, when I received his order to stop and form my company. I obeyed, and soon your father

came up, mounted on the colonel's horse, with another wound through his face and mouth, and which he thought the most dangerous and fatal, though it did not prove so.

The incidents of the battle are still fresh in my memory, but the events of the next two or three weeks I cannot distinctly remember. No doubt your father was decently buried with due solemnity, as the event made a deep impression in that region, as well as in the army. Much care was always taken, when it could be, to make the funeral services solemn and imposing.

Should it ever again be my fortune to visit Boston, I shall endeavor to find your residence, where your widowed mother found a home, and lived to a good old age. It would be a gratification in my old age to trace the lineaments of your father, still fresh in my mind, in the features of his son.

Very respectfully yours,
RUFUS McINTIRE.

IN MEMORIAM.

These little sketches of poetry, written soon after the death of the persons referred to, are not inserted here for any intrinsic value they may possess in themselves, but simply as mementos of departed friends.

✦✦✦✦✦

KATIE ADAMS DALRYMPLE.

Born in Dorchester, Mass. Feb. 13, 1851.
Died in Bradford, Mass. April 16, 1874.

Safely in her home above,
Rests our darling Katie now,
Sweetly rests in Jesus' love,
Earthly pains no more to know:
There to join the angel choirs,
Who upon mount Zion stand,
And with golden harps and lyres,
Praise the Lord—a happy band.

Though she felt 't was hard for one
Thus to part with friends so dear,

And death's river cross alone,
When life's morn was bright and clear.
Yet with sweet, confiding trust
In the Saviour's precious blood,
She the body gave to dust,
Spirit to the Just and Good.

Sadly do we miss her here,
Miss her cheerful, smiling face,
Miss her voice, its tones so dear,
Constantly, in every place.
Home has lost a treasure rare,
And the world has one less star;
Heaven has gained a jewel fair,
And the welcome sounded far.

Who would wish her back again,
All these mortal pains to bear?
Rather should we count it gain,
Earth to leave and meet her there:
Meet her where the skies are bright,
And unceasing pleasure flows;
In that land of pure delight,
Which no sin nor sorrow knows.

Roy Richmond Root.

Born in Georgetown, Mass. Sept. 30, 1873.
Died in Georgetown, Mass. June 8, 1876.

Gently as the summer breeze
Rustles through the leafy trees,
Sweetly as the music swells
Through the woodland hills and dells,
So he came, our darling boy,
Gentle, loving, little Roy.

Like a flower in perfect bloom.
Rich in beauty and perfume;
Like an angel from above,
Full of gentleness and love;
Such was he, our precious boy,
Loved and loving little Roy.

More and more his gentle ways,
In his life and childish plays;
In his every wish expressed,
And in every kiss impressed,
Bound our hearts, in love and joy,
To our gentle loving boy.

As the sun descends at night,
In a flood of golden light,
So he passed from mortal view,
To a life divinely new :
In that life of holy joy,
There we hope to meet our Roy.

MARY ELIZABETH DALRYMPLE.

Born in Gardner, Mass. Jan. 24, 1842.
Died in Haverhill, Mass. Dec. 28, 1876.

The Spring will come with its fragrant gales,
And birds return from a southern clime ;
The flowers will bloom on the hills and vales,
As fresh and fair as in former time :
But she has gone to return no more,
With God to dwell in the mansions bright,
And watch and wait on the other shore,
To welcome us to that world of light.

She loved the songs of the church below,
And now, we trust, in the choir above,
Her voice breaks forth in a sweeter flow,
To sing the song of redeeming love.
Who knows the joy of a ransomed soul,
When loved ones meet on the heavenly shore,
Where sin and death will have no control,
And mortal pains will be felt no more.

Death came to her in a stealthy way,
The spirit took at the midnight hour,
And left, alas, but a lump of clay,
No more of worth than a withered flower.
But God we know is a God of love,
And all He does is but just and right;
He reigns supreme on his throne above,
And crowns his own in the world of light.

TRUSTING AND HOPING.

One by one our friends depart
To the land of future rest,
While we oft with aching heart,
Yield to heaven's high behest.

Sad and lonely do we feel,
When we think of former days,
Scenes of youth that linger still,
Like the sun's departing rays.

But in faith and hope and trust,
Far beyond this world of pain,
With the spirits of the just,
There we hope to meet again;—

Meet in yonder world of light,
There to sin and stray no more,
But in raptures of delight,
Jesus on the throne adore.

"ONLY WAITING BY THE RIVER."

Only waiting by the river,
Waiting on the hither shore,
For the coming of the boatman,
List'ning for the dipping oar.

Weary with life's lengthened journey,
And its scenes of strife and blood,
Calmly waiting for the passage
To the land beyond the flood.

Though a fog lies on the river,
And sometimes obscures his sight,
Yet, full well the christian knoweth,
All beyond is clear and bright.

Friends and kindred, loved and loving,
Who have crossed that stream before,
Waiting stand to bid him welcome,
On that other, brighter shore.

Only waiting for the boatman,
Who will soon return again
For an aged, weary pilgrim,
Bowed with three-score years and ten.

[These hymns were written by W. H. D.]

www.ingramcontent.com/pod-product-compliance
Lightning Source LLC
Chambersburg PA
CBHW020146170426
43199CB00010B/917